1&2 Thessalonians

30 Daily Insights by **Sim Kay Tee**

Journey Through 1 & 2 Thessalonians
© 2022 by Sim Kay Tee
Published by Discovery House Publishing Singapore Pte. Ltd.
All rights reserved.

Our Daily Bread Publishing is affiliated
with Our Daily Bread Ministries.

Requests for permission to quote
from this book should be directed to:

Permissions Department
Our Daily Bread Publishing
P. O. Box 3566
Grand Rapids, MI 49501, USA

Or contact us by email at
permissionsdept@odb.org

All websites listed are accurate at the time of publication, but may change in the
future or cease to exist. The listing of the website references does not imply our
endorsement of the site's entire contents.

Cover design by Joshua Tan
Typeset by Lidya Jap

ISBN 978-1-913135-83-6

Printed in the United Kingdom
23 24 25 26 27 / 5 4 3 2 1

Foreword

The infant churches of the New Testament have been worthy models for churches desiring to grow their congregations. Some church growth experts have postulated, based on Acts 2:42–47, that every local assembly must have the characteristics of "WIFE" (Worship, Instruction in the Word, Fellowship, and Evangelism), as did the churches of apostolic times.

The apostle Paul is believed to have planted some 20 churches across the Roman world. Reading the letters he wrote to various churches presents a glimpse of first century church life. In particular, one of the churches Paul planted, the Thessalonian church, was acclaimed as a "model" church—hailed and commended for her "work produced by faith, [her] labour prompted by love, and [her] endurance inspired by hope in our Lord Jesus Christ" (1 Thessalonians 1:3; see also vv. 7–8). According to Paul, this trilogy of faith, love, and hope was a sign of their spiritual growth and maturity.

As we eagerly await the return of our Lord Jesus, let's continue to lead lives that are worthy of God and pleasing to Him (1 Thessalonians 2:12; 4:1). As the visible body of Jesus Christ, may we be known by our faithful work, loving deeds, and enduring hope.

To the founding members of
Bethesda Bedok Mission Home (1976),
Bethesda Bedok Mission Church (1988), and
Bethesda Pasir Ris Mission Church (1996),
who have pilgrimaged with me.

Soli Deo gloria,
Sim Kay Tee

We're glad you've decided to join us on a journey into a deeper relationship with Jesus Christ!

The *Journey Through* series is designed to help believers spend time with God in His Word, book by book. Each title is written by a faithful Bible teacher to help you read, reflect, and apply God's Word, a little bit at a time. It's a great accompaniment to be read alongside the Bible, as you dig deeper into God's Word. We trust the meditation on God's Word will draw you into a closer relationship with Him through our Lord and Saviour, Jesus Christ.

How to use this resource

READ: After reading and reflecting on the Bible verses, use the explanatory notes to help you understand the Scriptures in fresh ways.

REFLECT: Use the questions to consider how you could respond to God and His Word, letting Him change you from the inside out.

RECORD: Jot down your thoughts and responses in the space provided to keep a diary of your journey with the Lord.

An Overview

The Thessalonian church was born with the arrival of the apostle Paul and his co-evangelists Silas, Timothy, and Luke in Thessalonica (modern-day Thessaloniki), the capital of the Roman province of Macedonia. As was his usual practice, Paul began by preaching in the city's Jewish synagogue (Acts 17:1–4). This was followed by reaching out to the Gentiles, who "turned to God from idols to serve the living and true God" (1 Thessalonians 1:9).

The infant church in Thessalonica struggled with several challenges, including persecution, doubt, sin, and false teaching. Hence, Paul wrote them two letters after his departure from the city. In 1 Thessalonians, he commended the church for her faithful perseverance amid persecution, encouraged his hearers to live holy lives, and reassured them of the hope of Christ's second coming.

A few months after writing his first letter, Paul discovered from a report that several issues still plagued the church, affecting her life and unity. These included increasing persecution, false teaching about Jesus' return, and disruptive conduct within the church. The apostle thus wrote 2 Thessalonians, in which he sought to correct sinful behaviour and erroneous beliefs, reminding the church to hold fast to the right teaching as she awaited Christ's return.

Structure

1 Thessalonians 1	Commendation of Thessalonians' faith
1 Thessalonians 2–3	Paul addresses criticism of his actions and absence
1 Thessalonians 4–5	Reminder to avoid immoral conduct and to lead godly lives
2 Thessalonians 1	Encouragement to be worthy of God's calling
2 Thessalonians 2	Warning against false teaching about Jesus' return
2 Thessalonians 3	Warning against unruly disruptive conduct

Key Verse

May God himself, the God of peace, sanctify you through and through. May your whole spirit, soul and body be kept blameless at the coming of our Lord Jesus Christ. —1 Thessalonians 5:23

Read 1 Thessalonians 1:1

The atmosphere at the church's annual general meeting was adversarial. The founding pastor was furious with a young deacon who had questioned his motives in choosing to fund a certain programme. Standing up, he reproached the deacon. "Young man, how dare you speak to me like that?" he thundered. "I started this church 40 years ago. This is my church! I will do what I believe is best for my church!"

Having founded the church in Thessalonica, Paul faced similar accusations of selfish, insincere, and deceitful motives. His critics also questioned his sudden departure and continued absence from the city (see Acts 17:1–10). As these false accusations affected the church, Paul had to respond to the attacks on his integrity.

In his first letter to the Thessalonians, Paul includes a lengthy defence of his ministry (1 Thessalonians 2:1–3:10). He chooses not to assert apostolic authority despite having the right to do so (2:6). Moreover, he is careful not to claim *personal* ownership of the church he founded, unlike the pastor we met earlier.

Instead, Paul affirms that the church is "in God the Father and the Lord Jesus Christ" (1:1). In other words, the believers in Thessalonica "belong to God the Father and the Lord Jesus Christ" (v. 1, NLT). Through believing in Jesus Christ, the Thessalonians had become God's children and members of His family (John 1:12; Ephesians 2:19).

The Greek word for church, *ekklesia*, means "an assembly or a group of people gathered together". The same word was used to describe the riotous mob which attacked Paul in Ephesus (Acts 19:32). However, it soon took on a distinct Christian meaning, coming to denote a gathering of believers in Christ. Literally, *ekklesia* means "called out". In His grace and mercy, God has called us "out of darkness into his wonderful light" to be His chosen people, His special possession (1 Peter 2:9). We are "[God's] church, purchased with his own blood" (Acts 20:28, NLT).

Paul also includes Silas and Timothy as co-authors of the letter.

Silas, or Silvanus, was one of the two men esteemed as "leaders among the believers" in Jerusalem who were chosen as emissaries to convey the decision of the council at Jerusalem (Acts 15:22). He was also a prophet who encouraged and strengthened the believers, and even the apostle Peter esteemed him as "a faithful

brother" (v. 32; 1 Peter 5:12). As Paul's primary co-evangelist, Silas co-founded the church in Thessalonica (Acts 17:1–10).

Timothy was a young man whom Paul had met in Lystra at the start of his second missionary journey (Acts 16:1–5). He became a disciple of Paul, who called him "my true son in the faith" (1 Timothy 1:2). Timothy was often sent as Paul's personal representative to the New Testament churches, which spoke volumes of his pastoral gifts and abilities (see 1 Corinthians 4:17; Philippians 2:19–24).

After Paul was forced to leave Thessalonica, he sent Timothy there to strengthen the church. It was his protégé's report that prompted this letter (1 Thessalonians 3:2–6).

The first letter to the Thessalonians came from the church's pioneering pastors—three men who were well-known and highly esteemed. The church, however, belonged not to these human leaders, but to "God the Father and the Lord Jesus Christ" (1:1).

In your experience, do church leaders tend to have a strong sense of personal ownership over the churches they serve? In what ways could this be a good or bad thing?

What does it mean for you to "belong to God the Father and the Lord Jesus Christ" (1 Thessalonians 1:1, NLT)? How would belonging to Christ affect the way you live?

Day 2

Read 1 Thessalonians 1:2–3

The chairman of the board of elders had convened an emergency meeting to address the deteriorating state of the church. Its leaders had used various numerical "performance indicators" to measure the spiritual health of the church, such as worship attendance and financial giving, and the numbers were not good—both had plummeted to their lowest in the church's 60-year history.

I wonder how they would have assessed the Thessalonian church Paul had co-founded. Would Paul have seen and addressed such problems in a similar way? Or was his approach different?

Paul was a caring pastor. He had ministered in Thessalonica for several months, and after he was forced to leave the city abruptly, he continued his pastoral ministry by praying for the church continually (1 Thessalonians 1:2). To encourage the believers, Paul assured them that he held them close to his heart, praying for them earnestly and constantly (3:10). This was something he did for all his spiritual children.

Paul begins his letter by thanking God for the spiritual growth of the Thessalonian church and commending her members in three specific areas—their "faithful work",

"loving deeds", and "enduring hope" (1:3, NLT).

Faithful work: The Thessalonian believers were well known for their work resulting from their faith in God (v. 8). Their faithful and exemplary lives were motivated by God's unconditional love (v. 3). Elsewhere, Paul spoke of such work as "faith expressing itself through love" (Galatians 5:6).

Loving deeds: Loving is hard, and was not something the Thessalonian believers could naturally do. Rather, they had to learn to love and learn to love better. Paul would later note that they had "been taught by God to love each other" and would pray that their love would "increase and overflow" (1 Thessalonians 4:9; 3:12). It is no wonder that Paul called their work a "labour of love" (1:3, ESV).

Enduring hope: Paul intentionally affirms Christ's return at the end of each chapter in 1 Thessalonians (1:10; 2:19; 3:13; 4:15; 5:23). By praising the Thessalonian believers' endurance, Paul was acknowledging their faithfulness, thus encouraging them to continue leading holy lives as they waited for Christ to return (3:13; 5:23).

For Paul, the measure of a church growing and maturing

in the faith was not in numbers, but in faithful work, loving deeds, and enduring hope.

Can attendance numbers at services (and prayer meetings) or financial giving statistics be considered as good measures of a church's growth and maturity? Why or why not?

Would "faithful work, loving deeds, and enduring hope" (1 Thessalonians 1:3, NLT) be appropriate ways to measure the progress of your home church? Why or why not?

Read 1 Thessalonians 1:4–10

"Which church in the New Testament stands out as the model for us to emulate today?" This question was asked at a church growth seminar I attended.

It was no surprise that not a single attendee mentioned the conflict-ridden and divided church at Corinth. As expected, everyone pointed to the infant church in Jerusalem, whose exemplary attributes were described in Acts 2:42–47. To the apostle Paul, the church in Thessalonica was a model church. That's why he commended them as "a model to all the believers in Macedonia and Achaia" (1 Thessalonians 1:7).

Why did Paul call her a model church? In what ways can this church be an example to believers today?

As we read previously, the church in Thessalonica was characterised by faithful work, loving deeds, and enduring hope (v. 3, NLT). Her members were carrying out the Great Commission and making an impact on their community with God's Word. They faithfully and boldly proclaimed the good news to people everywhere, even beyond their own borders. As Paul put it, "the Lord's message rang out from you not only in Macedonia and Achaia—your faith in God has become known everywhere" (v. 8).

The Thessalonians led such radically transformed lives that people could see and feel the difference. Their godly and Christ-like conduct left a deep impression on those around them (vv. 6–7). Indeed, it could be said that they had "turned the world upside down" (Acts 17:6, ESV). The Thessalonians were a model church because they served the Lord faithfully, loved each other deeply, and longed to see the Lord at His second coming (1 Thessalonians 1:9–10).

In short, they excelled in faith, hope, and love—the three cardinal virtues of the Christian life, and the three greatest signs of salvation.

Paul would stress the importance of this trilogy again when he instructed the Thessalonians to dress themselves for battle, to put on "*faith* and *love* as a breastplate, and the *hope* of salvation as a helmet" (5:8; emphasis added, see Day 17). In the New Testament, the trilogy of faithful work, loving deeds, and enduring hope is a mark of the maturing church (see Colossians 1:4-5; Hebrews 10:22–24).

As believers in Jesus, we too would do well to seek to excel in faith, love, and hope. Why? As Paul notes, these virtues are critical and eternal: "Three things will last forever—faith,

hope, and love—and the greatest of these is love" (1 Corinthians 13:13, NLT).

Paul praised the Thessalonians for becoming "imitators of us and of the Lord" (1 Thessalonians 1:6). Whose imitation of Christ is an encouragement to you? How? Why?

Would you consider yourself a "model" Christian? Why or why not? In what areas would you want people (such as friends or your children, if you are a parent) to imitate you?

Read 1 Thessalonians 2:1–6

"Pastor accused of financial misappropriation". "Church elder convicted of accounting fraud". "Pastor guilty of cheating elderly wealthy widow". Headlines like these tell of an insidious sin that has plagued the church of Christ since the beginning.

In the ancient world, itinerant philosophers and teachers would come into town to deliver lectures. Just like today, some of these speakers were pretenders who deceitfully used religion as "a means to financial gain" (1 Timothy 6:5; see also Titus 1:11; 2 Peter 2:3, 15). (Of course, this is different from giving a worker what he rightfully earns, as 1 Timothy 5:18 notes.)

Paul's detractors had accused him of deceitful motives in starting a church in Thessalonica, the prosperous provincial capital of Macedonia. The apostle, they charged, was quick to abandon his followers the moment his own life was threatened because his sole purpose had been to gain praise and money (1 Thessalonians 2:5–6).

Paul now addresses these charges. He explains his motives, abrupt departure, and continued absence; he defends his integrity and ministry, and clarifies his motivation, message, and methods.

As a minister of the gospel, the apostle was always careful to ensure that his conduct and motives were completely above board. He constantly emphasised the necessity and priority of transparency, sincerity, honesty, and accountability in his life and ministry. And he made sure that his message was never adulterated, his motives never impure, and his methods never improper.

How did he do this?

First, Paul made himself fully accountable to other believers—his life was always an open book. In this letter, he appeals to his readers' personal knowledge of how he had lived when he was with them, saying, "*You know* how we lived among you for your sake." Six times he reminds them: "*You know*" (2:1, 2, 5, 11; 3:3, 4; emphases added). And he stresses: "*You can see* we were not preaching with any deceit or impure motives or trickery" (2:3, NLT; emphasis added).

Second, and more importantly, Paul was always answerable to God, who entrusted him with the mission to preach the good news. His single purpose was "to please God, not people", for "He alone examines the motives of our hearts" (v. 4, NLT). Since Paul knew that there could be no pretending before God, he could say again, with confidence, "You know we never used flattery, nor did we put on a mask to cover up greed—God is our witness" (v. 5).

Elsewhere, Paul also wrote: "Unlike so many, we do not peddle the word of God for profit. On the contrary, in Christ we speak before God with sincerity, as those sent from God" (2 Corinthians 2:17). Like Paul, may we also be able to say confidently, "You are witnesses, and so is God, of how holy, righteous and blameless we were among you who believed" (1 Thessalonians 2:10). Unlike the many charlatans who preach for personal profit, let us live transparently and with integrity, knowing that God and our fellow believers will certainly hold us to account.

Read what 2 Corinthians 4:1–2, Ephesians 5:3–5, and 1 Peter 5:2 say about integrity in Christian conduct and service. How do you measure up to these standards?

Paul says that God "tests our hearts" (1 Thessalonians 2:4). How might God's unceasing scrutiny guard today's Christian leaders against unworthy motives and actions? How could it change the way you live?

Day 5

Read 1 Thessalonians 2:7–13

Having defended his ministry and explained his message, motives, and methods (1 Thessalonians 2:1–6), Paul offers another defence of himself. This time, he highlights his role as a pastor (vv. 7–13). The Thessalonian believers were Paul's spiritual sons and daughters; he had nurtured these infant believers until strong opposition forced him away from them (Acts 17:1–10).

What kind of pastor and spiritual parent was Paul?

Because of his severity towards false teachers and sinful conduct in his letters, Paul has often come across as hardhearted and lacking empathy and compassion. His affectionate and tender side is often overshadowed by his no-nonsense approach. However, in this passage, Paul displays parental vulnerability.

First, he shows a feminine aspect, showering his hearers with motherly tenderness. "We were like a mother feeding and caring for her own children," he says with the gentle concern of a nursing mother. "We loved you so much that we shared with you not only God's Good News but our own lives, too" (1 Thessalonians 2:7–8, NLT).

Then, he speaks with the paternal concern of a nurturing father, urging his spiritual children to lead holy lives. "We dealt with each of you as a father deals with his own children, encouraging, comforting and urging you to live lives worthy of God" (vv. 11-12).

Paul expected his spiritual children to live in a manner that God would consider worthy of himself. Biblical expositor Alexander Maclaren notes that this is the whole law of Christian conduct in a nutshell. He observes: "There may be many detailed commandments, but they can all be deduced from this one. Instead of regulations, very many and very dry, we have a principle which needs thought and sympathy in order to apply it, and is to be carried out by the free action of our own judgments."[1]

"To live lives worthy of God" means ensuring that everything we do— our words, actions, and thoughts—is consistent with our heavenly Father. We are to "follow God's example . . . as dearly loved children and live a life of love" (Ephesians 5:1–2; see also Matthew 5:48; 1 Peter 1:14–15). We are to

become more and more like His Son Jesus Christ (see Romans 8:29; 2 Corinthians 3:18). And we are to "be holy in everything [we] do, just as God who chose [us] is holy" (1 Peter 1:15, NLT).

To live worthy lives, we need God's Word, for it has power to transform lives. As Paul notes in 1 Thessalonians 2:13, the Bible is "not . . . a human word, but . . . it actually is, the word of God, which is indeed at work in you who believe". We need to receive, believe, and live by God's Word (see Deuteronomy 32:46–47; Psalm 119:9–16).

This is a worthy goal for parents, both biological and spiritual—to desire that their children live fruitful lives that honour and please the Lord in every way (see Colossians 1:10).

How would you describe Paul's relationship with the Thessalonian believers? What can you learn from Paul about extending pastoral care to others?

How might you contribute to the spiritual development of your biological or spiritual children? What is one thing you could do to help them know God better?

1 "Walking Worthily", Alexander MacLaren's Expositions of Holy Scripture, 1 Thessalonians 2:12, StudyLight.org. Accessed from https://www.studylight.org/commentaries/mac/1-thessalonians-2.html

Day 6

Read 1 Thessalonians 2:14–3:5

Recently, I came across the heartwarming story of an abandoned baby saved in a miraculous way. A teenage mother had buried her newborn under a layer of dirt in a field, but a dog found the baby on the very same day and alerted its owner, who was a farmer.[2] Sadly, however, this is most unusual—many abandoned babies die before they can be rescued.

Abandonment was the key charge laid against Paul. His enemies accused him of deserting the infant church in Thessalonica just as she was beginning to undergo persecution, and then refusing to return to help. In 1 Thessalonians 2:1–6, Paul responded by reminding the Thessalonian believers how faithful a preacher he had been to them, and how loving a pastor-parent he had been for them (vv. 7–13). In today's passage, Paul goes on to explain his sudden departure and continued absence.

Abrupt abandonment: Paul was called to be an apostle to the Gentiles. But wherever he went, there were Jews who opposed his efforts (v. 16; see also Acts 13:50; 14:2, 19; 17:13). In Thessalonica, some local Jews had instigated a riot against Paul and the church, as described in Acts 17:5–9 and as Paul recalls in 1 Thessalonians 2:14–15. His continued presence in the city would have brought about yet more vicious persecution upon the infant church, so he left to prevent further harm from befalling them.

Continued absence: Paul had earlier addressed the Thessalonian believers as his beloved "brothers and sisters" (1:4). Repeating this familial metaphor, he now writes of being "orphaned by being separated from you for a short time (in person, not in thought)" (2:17). Paul's family has been torn apart, but he cherishes the believers in his heart though physically separated from them.

Paul also reveals that he had made "every effort" to see the Thessalonians again—"We wanted to come to you—certainly I, Paul, did, again and again" (vv. 17–18). But these repeated attempts to return were blocked by circumstances which he attributed to the devil (v. 18). His absence, he emphasises, was certainly not due to lack of love or effort.

Assurance and priorities: Having explained his departure and absence, Paul assures the Thessalonian believers that he would not abandon them (3:1–5). To return and teach God's Word to them, in fact, remained of primary concern and priority—"Night and day we pray

most earnestly that we may see you again and supply what is lacking in your faith" (v. 10).

Paul demonstrated the importance of this priority to him by sending another teacher to the believers, who would "strengthen and encourage [them] in [their] faith, so that no one would be unsettled by these trials" (vv. 2–3). The man sent, Timothy, was no junior worker or novice Bible teacher, but an esteemed member of Paul's pastoral and teaching team—"our brother and co-worker in God's service" (v. 2).

Although Paul had to leave Thessalonica in haste and was unable to return, in fervent love, he did his best to ensure that the believers were cared for spiritually.

What is one prayer you could say for your (biological or spiritual) children this week?

Are you helping or mentoring someone whom you cannot meet in person? Think of a few creative ways to stay in touch and ensure that he or she continues to grow in the faith.

---

[2] "Dog rescues baby buried alive in field in Thailand", *BBC*, 17 May 2019. Accessed from https://www.bbc.com/news/world-asia-48311028

Day 7

Read 1 Thessalonians 3:6–8

Joseph Bayly, a Christian author who lost three young sons to disease, was intimately acquainted with suffering and pain. In *The View from a Hearse*, he writes about bereavement and the people who came to comfort him.

"I was sitting, torn by grief," he recalls. "Someone came and talked to me of God's dealings, of why it happened, of hope beyond the grave. He talked constantly, he said things I knew were true. I was unmoved, except to wish he'd go away. He finally did.

"Another came and sat beside me. He didn't talk. He didn't ask leading questions. He just sat beside me for an hour or more, listened when I said something, answered briefly, prayed simply, left. I was moved. I was comforted. I hated to see him go."[3]

The Thessalonians, too, had good memories of Paul's visit. Undoubtedly, they would have hated to see him go. They yearned to see Paul again, as much as Paul himself longed to see them again (1 Thessalonians 3:6). Timothy, whom Paul sent to the city in his place, probably ministered to the Thessalonians for a couple of months before returning to Paul in Corinth (see Acts 18:5).

And what good news Timothy had for Paul! His reports of the Thessalonian believers' "faith and love" brought great joy and relief to Paul (1 Thessalonians 3:6). Paul had intended to encourage and strengthen his spiritual children in their faith, but now, he humbly acknowledges that it was the Thessalonians who were the ones encouraging and strengthening him: "We have been greatly encouraged in the midst of our troubles and suffering, dear brothers and sisters, because you have remained strong in your faith" (v. 7, NLT).

Encouragement was important to Paul. Wherever he went, Paul faced strong opposition and persecution by those who wanted to stop his evangelistic mission to the Gentiles. He was brutally beaten and imprisoned in Philippi (see 2:2; see also Acts 16:19–24), forced to flee Thessalonica (see 1 Thessalonians 2:14–15), and pursued all the way to Berea (see Acts 17:13). Clearly, if anyone needed encouragement— lots of it—it was Paul himself.

Now, the good news from Timothy of the Thessalonians' faith gave Paul the boost he needed, rejuvenating and energising him. With deep gratitude

to God, Paul rejoiced: "It gives us new life to know that you are standing firm in the Lord. How we thank God for you! Because of you we have great joy as we enter God's presence" (1 Thessalonians 3:8–9, NLT).

Who needs encouragement?

Everyone. Even the great apostle Paul needed encouragement. Three times in this letter, he urged his hearers to "encourage one another" (4:18; 5:11, 14). His words echo those penned by the writer of the letter to the Hebrew believers, who were battered and discouraged: "Encourage one another daily, as long as it is called 'Today'" (Hebrews 3:13).

[3] Joseph Bayly, *The View from A Hearse* (David C. Cook Publishing Co., 1973), 55–56.

Is there someone you can encourage today? What would you do to encourage him or her?

Has anyone encouraged you this past week? How did they encourage you? Encourage them too by telling them about how they encouraged you, and how much you appreciate it.

Day 8

Read 1 Thessalonians 3:9–13

We can't know for certain the exact number of churches Paul planted during his lifetime, but the apostle visited and brought the gospel to more than 50 cities during his missionary journeys.[4]

Paul, however, was no "touch and go" evangelist. Having brought the Thessalonians to faith in Jesus, he assumed personal responsibility for nurturing their spiritual growth. He prayed constantly and "most earnestly" for their maturity, for this was his unwavering commitment (1 Thessalonians 3:10; see also 1:2–3). To the apostle, praying for his spiritual children was a delight, not a burden, because he treasured them as members of his own family. They were his hope, his glory, and his joy (3:9; see also 2:19–20).

In today's passage, we see Paul praying for three things.

First, he prays that he might get to visit the Thessalonian believers again, in order to nurture and equip them, and "supply what is lacking in [their] faith" (3:10). While Paul had previously told them how difficult it was to visit them (see 2:18), his desire may have been fulfilled some 5 years later during his third missionary journey, when he managed to visit Macedonia, the provincial capital of which was Thessalonica (see Acts 20:1–5).

Second, he prays for the Thessalonian believers' continued growth and maturity, and that their "love for one another and for all people grow and overflow" (1 Thessalonians 3:12, NLT). By this time, they were already "known everywhere" for their "labour prompted by love", but Paul hoped that this love would not only "increase" but also "overflow"—not only for fellow Christians, but also for everyone else (1:3, 8; 3:12).

Third, he prays that the Thessalonian believers would remain steadfast and faithful, "blameless and holy in the presence of our God and Father when our Lord Jesus comes" (3:13; see also 2 Peter 3:11, 14). Paul reminded his hearers about the Lord's return, and how they ought to live holy lives until then. As Bible teacher Warren Wiersbe observes: "Again, it is the return of Jesus Christ that motivates the believer to live a holy life. Our Lord's return is also a source of stability in the Christian life. Where there is stability, there can be sanctity, and where there is holiness, there is assurance. The two go together."[5]

Paul's prayer shows us how to pray for fellow believers— not only for new believers, but for *all* believers. We can pray his prayer for ourselves too—

that we would seek opportunities to minister to fellow believers, grow in our intimacy with God, and love people as Jesus does. Let us pray that our lives might be holy before God our Father and a watching world.

4 "All cities visited by Apostle Paul map". *Bible Study*. Accessed from https://www.biblestudy.org/maps/apostle-paul-all-cities-visited-map.html

5 Notes on 1 Thessalonians 3:10, Warren W. Wiersbe (ed.), *The Wiersbe Study Bible* (Thomas Nelson, 2019).

Read Paul's prayer for the Thessalonian believers again (1 Thessalonians 3:9–13). What were his priorities for them?

How might Paul's prayer guide your own prayers for the people you love, or for those to whom you are ministering?

Day 9

Read 1 Thessalonians 4:1–7

Suppose you are writing a personal letter to a close friend whom you had not contacted for some time. What would you say? Perhaps you would give him an update on your life, family, and work. But would you warn him to stay away from all sexual sin and live a morally pure life? Would you warn him about God's punishment? Probably not. And you probably wouldn't write to tell him not to commit adultery either, since it would likely be considered out of line.

This is why what Paul writes next is surprising. With strong words and warning of God's judgment, he instructs the Thessalonian believers to stay away from sexual sin of any kind, to control their lusts, and not to harm others by committing adultery (1 Thessalonians 4:3–6).

Such a warning would have been necessary and timely for the church in Corinth because sexual immorality was a major problem there (see 1 Corinthians 5:1–2). But here in 1 Thessalonians, this warning seems out of place and unnecessary. Paul had just commended the believers in Thessalonica for their exemplary and holy lives, calling them "a model to all the believers in Macedonia and Achaia" (1 Thessalonians 1:7). So why would he write with such severity?

First, we need to understand the place where the believers lived. Thessalonica was a large and prosperous city plagued by the same social and moral ills that characterise every cosmopolitan city—consumerism, materialistic indulgence, greed, debauchery, lust, prostitution, and sexual promiscuity. Temple prostitution was officially sanctioned by fertility cult religions, giving rise to Thessalonica's notorious and pervasive immorality.[6] Such were the temptations faced by the Thessalonian believers on a daily basis.

Second, we should recognise Paul's two-pronged approach to teaching in general. On the one hand, he would get involved when things were falling apart, dealing decisively with immediate problems in the church, such as false teachings about Christ's return (see 4:13–18). On the other hand, Paul would also speak when things were going well: "We instructed you how to live in order to please God, as in fact you are living" (v. 1). When the believers were on the right path, Paul would challenge them to keep at it—and to do better. Twice, he exhorts them "to do . . . more and more" (vv. 1, 10).

Paul's words in today's passage reflect his overall teaching strategy—

to teach the whole counsel of God, "the word of God in its fullness" (Colossians 1:25). For "all Scripture is God-breathed and is useful for teaching, rebuking, correcting and training in righteousness" (2 Timothy 3:16).

Paul's approach gives us a pattern to emulate in helping fellow believers to lead worthy lives. Let us teach "everyone with all wisdom, so that we may present everyone fully mature in Christ" (Colossians 1:28).

What are some modern day temptations that you face on a daily basis? How do you guard yourself against them?

How would knowing God's Word protect you from such temptations?

[6] John Stott, *The Message of 1 & 2 Thessalonians – The Gospel and the End of Time* (IVP, 1991), 81.

Read 1 Thessalonians 4:1–2

While teaching a youth discipleship class, I asked the youngsters to set a goal for themselves for the next 12 months. One young man said that he wanted to read through the whole Bible within a year. Another said he would attend church on Sunday regularly. A third resolved to share the gospel with one person every week.

While all these goals were good and noble, in today's passage, Paul urges believers to focus on just one goal: "to live in order to please God" (1 Thessalonians 4:1).

Christianity is a love relationship. The main point and characteristic of such a relationship is to please the one we love. To please God, therefore, lies at the root of our discipleship, and is the guiding principle and goal for every follower of Christ.

"To live in order to please God" gives us an ethical guideline that is practical for everyday living. It rescues us from the legalism and rigidity of a Pharisee-like approach that tries to entrench our Christian life in a set of rules, in a list of dos and don'ts. Instead, we need only to ask ourselves: "Will God be pleased with me if I do this?"

In 1 Thessalonians 2:4, Paul had established this principle by saying, "We are not trying to please people but God." How do we please God in all that we do? By imitating the Lord Jesus, who had the same goal: "I seek not to please myself but him who sent me . . . I always do what pleases him" (John 5:30; 8:29). To please God is to live like Christ, for what Christ did always pleased the Father.

There are three things to remember about pleasing God.

First, the desire to please God is not something we have by our own will and strength. As Paul notes in Romans 8:8, "those who are in the realm of the flesh cannot please God." Instead, "God is working in you, giving you the desire and the power to do what pleases him" (Philippians 2:13, NLT). We must therefore pray that God our great Shepherd will "equip [us] with everything good for doing his will, and may he work in us what is pleasing to him" (Hebrews 13:21).

Second, pleasing God is much more than just obeying Him. The story of the prophet Jonah shows us that it is possible to obey the Lord without pleasing Him (see Jonah 3:3; 4:1–4). It is *loving* obedience that

will please the Father. Like Jesus, let us declare: "I love the Father and do exactly what my Father has commanded me" (John 14:31).

Third, pleasing God is not a one-time effort, nor can it be confined to one specific aspect of life. Rather, this endeavour permeates our whole being. One ought to love Him "with all your heart and with all your soul and with all your mind" (Matthew 22:37). In 1 Thessalonians 4:1, Paul goes even further: "Now we ask you and urge you in the Lord Jesus to do this more and more."

This, then, is the nature of a mature Christian—to be willing to surrender more and more of his life, until all of his being pleases God.

How would asking, "Will God be pleased with me if I do this?" affect your decision-making and your actions each day?

What personal goal can you set that would please the Lord? What are some things you have done or are doing that might be displeasing to Him? Why would He be displeased by these things?

Read 1 Thessalonians 4:3–5

nternet pornography is one of the scourges of our times. According to some reports, more than 30,000 people watch pornography online every second. Studies also show that Christians are no less vulnerable to pornography than non-Christians, with many saying that they were first exposed to such content before the age of 12.[7] Technology has made it far too easy for anybody—even children—to access pornography.

How, then, do we live the Christian life in this lust-filled world? In 1 Thessalonians 4:3, Paul tells us that "it is God's will that you should be sanctified".

We often think of "God's will" as something that He demands of us. But the Greek word for "will", *thélēma*, is not to be understood as a demand. Rather, as one definition notes: "When it denotes God's will, it signifies His gracious disposition toward something."[8] Doing God's will or being in God's will is what God desires of us. This honours Him, and He rejoices for us when we do His will.

"Sanctified" sounds like a big theological word, but it simply means being "set apart or consecrated or dedicated". It means being set apart, for God, to be distinct from the people of this world—to be made separate from evil. God is pleased when we lead holy lives even when we are surrounded by promiscuity and immorality.

Paul also tells us to "avoid sexual immorality" (v. 3). On this, biblical commentator John Stott writes: "'Avoid' is too weak a word."[9] The New Living Translation (NLT) renders the phrase as "stay away from all sexual sin", while the J. B. Phillips New Testament translation does so with even greater force, calling on us to execute "a clean cut with sexual immorality".

When it comes to sexual temptation and sexual sin, we must keep a safe distance. In fact, Paul exhorts us to take flight in the opposite direction. "Flee from sexual immorality!" he says in 1 Corinthians 6:18. The Greek word for "flee" is *pheúgō*, which means "to take to flight in order to seek safety".[10] Because of the urgency and severity of the danger, we are to run away as fast as we can. Joseph, when tempted by Potiphar's wife, did not stay around to fight off the temptation. Instead, he "ran out of the house" (Genesis 39:12). We must flee because of our weakness and sinfulness; we have to accept that there are times when "the spirit is willing, but the flesh is weak" (Matthew 26:41).

By thinking that we can stay put and fight temptation with our own strength, we would be foolishly over-estimating ourselves and our ability to resist. We would also be grossly underestimating the power of sexual temptation to entice and entrap us (see Proverbs 6:27–28). It is unwise to stay and try to fight it out. The Bible reminds us to "flee", and not to linger and resist (1 Corinthians 6:18). This is how we can maintain purity in an impure culture.

Read what Proverbs 5:8, 1 Corinthians 6:18, and 2 Timothy 2:22 say about dealing with sexual temptation. Why do you think Scripture tells us to "flee"? How can you do this in practical ways?

Paul says that it is God's will that we should be sanctified (1 Thessalonians 4:3). What are some things you could do to live a sexually pure life?

[7] "Internet Pornography by the Numbers; A Significant Threat to Society", *WebRoot*. Accessed from https://www.webroot.com/us/en/resources/tips-articles/internet-pornography-by-the-numbers.

John Biggs, "The annual PornHub year in review tells us what we're really looking at online", *TechCrunch*, Dec 14, 2018. Accessed from https://techcrunch.com/2018/12/13/the-annual-pornhub-year-in-review-tells-us-what-were-really-looking-at-online/

"Christians and Online Porn", *Enough Is Enough*. Accessed from https://enough.org/stats_christians_online_porn

[8] Spiros Zodhiates (ed.), *The Complete Word Study Dictionary: New Testament* (AMG Publishers, 1992). Quoted in "Will – Thelema (Greek Word Study)", *Precept Austin*. Accessed from https://www.preceptaustin.org/will_thelema

[9] John Stott, *The Gospel and the End of Time – The Message of 1 & 2 Thessalonians*, (IVP, 1991), 82.

[10] "1 Corinthians 6:18 Commentary", *Precept Austin*. Accessed from https://www.preceptaustin.org/1corinthians_618_commentary

Day 12

Read 1 Thessalonians 4:3–8

God created mankind as sexual beings—"male and female he created them" (Genesis 1:27). His first command to mankind involved the sexual act between a man and a woman—"be fruitful and increase in number" (v. 28; see also 2:24–25). Sex was part of the creation that God had called "very good" (1:31). As such, sexual intimacy between a husband and wife, as God originally intended, is good and holy!

Paul says that to live a holy life, we must "learn to control [our] own body in a way that is holy and honourable" (1 Thessalonians 4:4). **Controlling our own desires and cravings—sexual or otherwise—is something that we all must learn to do, as the Spirit helps us.** And this mastering of our own bodies, Paul says in Colossians 3:5, must include the severe act of putting to death whatever belongs to our "earthly nature", which includes sexual immorality, impurity, lust, and evil desires.

The Greek words for the phrase "to control your own body" can also mean "to live with your own wife" or "to acquire a wife". In fact, the Revised Standard Version and the Good News Translation both render it as "take a wife for yourself" and "live with your wife".

Before the fall of Adam and Eve in Genesis 3, God had purposed marriage for procreation and partnership (see Genesis 1:28; 2:18). After the fall, marriage took on a third purpose—a preventive against sexual immorality. "Because there is so much sexual immorality, each man should have his own wife, and each woman should have her own husband," Paul told the Corinthian church, and concluded: "It's better to marry than to burn with lust" (1 Corinthians 7:2, 9, NLT).

At the same time, anyone seeking marriage must do so "in a way that is holy and honourable, not in passionate lust like the pagans, who do not know God" (1 Thessalonians 4:4–5). We are not to treat marriage as a thing to feed our lustful cravings. Lust is sexual desire without the commitment to honour, cherish, love, and respect one's marriage partner; it treats him or her as a mere object for personal sexual gratification.

Paul lists three motivations for loving our marriage partner in a holy and honourable way.

First, he warns that "the Lord will punish all those who commit such sins" (v. 6). Sexual purity in marriage must be held in high regard. As Hebrews 13:4 makes clear: "Marriage should be honoured by all, and the

marriage bed kept pure, for God will judge the adulterer and all the sexually immoral."

Second, God himself calls us to lead holy lives (1 Thessalonians 4:7). Holiness lies at the core of our salvation—2 Timothy 1:9 stresses that God "has saved us and called us to a holy life", and Ephesians 5:25–27 declares that Jesus "gave himself up for [the church] to make her holy . . . without stain or wrinkle or any other blemish, but holy and blameless". 1 Peter 1:15–16, too, reminds us that we are to be holy because God himself is holy. And sexual purity is one aspect of holiness, which is God's will for us (1 Thessalonians 4:3, 7).

Third, the Holy Spirit living in us must transform how we use our bodies, motivating us to live in a way that pleases God (v. 8). As 1 Corinthians 6:19–20 stresses: "Your bodies are temples of the Holy Spirit, who is in you, whom you have received from God . . . Therefore honour God with your bodies."

Paul further warns that "anyone who rejects this instruction does not reject a human being but God" (1 Thessalonians 4:8). This is how seriously God takes our sexual purity!

Read 1 Thessalonians 4:4–8 again. What guidelines did Paul set for sexual behaviour? How could you apply these guidelines in practical ways?

What would these biblical guidelines mean in today's context? How might we establish and maintain biblical standards for sexual purity without becoming unnecessarily puritanical or prudish?

Day 13

Read 1 Thessalonians 4:9–10

Over the past few days, we looked at Paul's call to believers to live in way that would please God, as well as the importance of practising sexual purity in an immoral and decadent world (see 1 Thessalonians 4:3–8). We were reminded that all Christians are called to lead holy lives, including living a sexually pure life.

But that is not all. Leading a holy life also means loving our brothers and sisters in Christ (see vv. 9–10).

Hours before going to the cross, Jesus gave His disciples a new commandment: "Love one another. As I have loved you, so you must love one another" (John 13:34). In a way, this instruction to love others was not new. In their Law, the Jews were commanded to love their neighbours in the same way they loved themselves (see Leviticus 19:18, 34). Jesus himself spoke often of this Mosaic standard (see Matthew 19:19; Luke 10:27). What was new here was that Jesus was introducing a *new, radical standard of loving*. The Living Bible translation succinctly captures Jesus' new commandment: "Love each other *just as much as I love you*" (John 13:34, TLB; emphasis added).

How much does Jesus love us? The answer: utterly and "to the end" of His very life (John 13:1). When

He laid down His life at the cross, Jesus "showed [us] the full extent of his love", as the NLT footnote for this verse puts it. Jesus' love is an unending, all-embracing, sacrificial love. To love *as Jesus loves* reframes the old commandment with a new standard of love, set by Jesus' own example.

Loving others as Jesus loves is indisputable proof that we are His disciples. Jesus said, "By this everyone will know that you are my disciples, if you love one another" (John 13:35). 1 John 3:10, too, observes that the children of God are revealed by their capacity to love, since God's children do what is right and love their brothers and sisters. But Paul also stresses that the ability to love is not something we can do by our natural will, because it belongs to the realm of the divine. We can love, he says, only because we "have been taught by God to love each other" (1 Thessalonians 4:9).

The Thessalonian church's love, like Jesus' love, had no bounds. Paul rejoiced in her love for "all of God's family throughout Macedonia" (v. 10). Although she was herself facing persecution, she gave financial aid generously and sacrificially to believers in other parts of Macedonia (see 2 Corinthians 8:1–5). Is it any

wonder that Paul commends her for being a model to all believers in Macedonia and Achaia?

What did Paul mean when he said that the Thessalonian believers had been "taught by God to love each other" (1 Thessalonians 4:9)? How did God teach them? How has God taught you to love?

How do you love others as you love yourself? How do you love others as Jesus has loved you?

Day 14

Read 1 Thessalonians 4:11–12

Paul has been urging the Thessalonians believers to lead holy lives, particularly in the aspect of sexual purity (see 1 Thessalonians 4:3–8), and to love others as Jesus has loved us (see vv. 9–10). Today, Paul considers a third way to please God: "to lead a quiet life"—that is, to live harmoniously and honourably (v. 11).

Most of the Thessalonian believers did love one another (v. 9). But there was a group of believers who were not showing such love for their brothers and sisters in Christ. Some of them abused the generosity of the community—instead of working for their own living, they lived off the kindness of others. Not only were these idlers and freeloaders lazy and unwilling to work, they also became busybodies and gossipers, always trying to intrude into the private lives of their brethren (see 5:14; 2 Thessalonians 3:11).

Paul now instructs these people "to live a quiet life, minding your own business and working with your hands", so that they would "not need to depend on others". Only then, he notes, "people who are not believers will respect the way you live" (1 Thessalonians 4:11–12, NLT). Evidently, their laziness and gossiping had diminished their Christian witness.

Paul accords dignity to hard work. Work is man's original vocation. It is a blessing from the Lord, and there is therefore dignity in working hard for a living (see Genesis 2:15; Ecclesiastes 2:24, 5:19). Some people are unable to work and need help from others, and we should support them. But those who are able to work, yet do not, are not acting in brotherly love. Working to sustain ourselves and our family is the right and loving thing to do.

Moreover, a self-supporting person would be able to contribute to the community's support for the genuinely needy. In Ephesians 4:28, for example, Paul specifically encourages hard work so that we would "have something to share with those in need". Demonstrating love in this way can win the respect of believers and unbelievers alike.

And, as he always did, Paul was leading by example. Earlier, he had referred to his own work ethic, reminding the Thessalonian believers "how hard we worked among you . . . to earn a living so that we would not be a burden to any of you as we preached God's Good News to you" (1 Thessalonians 2:9, NLT).

While Paul was entitled to seek support from those whom he ministered to, he chose not to. Instead, he worked hard as a tentmaker to support himself (see Acts 18:3; 20:34). Preaching the gospel "free of charge", he explained in 1 Corinthians 9:11–18, helped him to avoid being accused of financially profiting from the gospel, ensuring that money would not get in the way of the message. Paul didn't want to burden the people or hinder God's work.

Thus, Paul was able to instruct the troublemakers to be socially responsible—to stop gossiping and meddling in others' personal lives, and to be financially responsible—to work hard for a living and not depend on others. This problem, unfortunately, could not be resolved, and Paul would have to deal with the freeloaders again in 2 Thessalonians 3:6–15 (see Days 29 and 30).

Why was Paul so concerned about idlers and believers who refused to work?

Reflect on 1 Thessalonians 4:12. What does your attitude towards work and the way you work say about your faith? How might your work ethic affect your Christian witness?

What did Paul teach concerning the church's support for those who do God's work? Read 1 Corinthians 9:4–14, Galatians 6:6–7, and 1 Timothy 5:17–18.

Day 15

Read 1 Thessalonians 4:13–18

nuka, a 27-year-old polar bear who was the star attraction at the Singapore Zoo, was very sick. He was not responding to treatment, and his carers felt that any further treatment, or allowing nature to take its course, would prolong his suffering. So, in April 2018, Singapore's last polar bear was put to "sleep" on compassionate grounds.[11]

In the Bible, "sleep" is used as a euphemism for physical death (see, for example, Acts 7:60; 13:36). Jesus spoke of those who died as "sleeping" (Matthew 9:24; John 11:11–13). And there will be a day when "multitudes who sleep in the dust of the earth will awake" (Daniel 12:2; see also John 5:28–29).

For Christians, "sleep" is more than just a euphemism to cushion the brutality of death and permanent separation from loved ones. Rather, it reflects the spiritual reality and future hope that those "who have fallen asleep in [Jesus]" will awake to everlasting life and "be with the Lord for ever" (1 Thessalonians 4:14, 17).

Paul makes it clear that Jesus "died and rose again" (v. 14)—the word "sleep" is not applied to Him. Hebrews 2:9, too, says that Jesus "suffered death, so that by the grace of God he might taste death for everyone", while Romans 4:25 notes

that "he was delivered over to death for our sins and was raised to life for our justification".

Christ's resurrection thus guarantees our resurrection (see 1 Corinthians 6:16; 15:13–24). We have Jesus' promise: "I am the resurrection and the life. Anyone who believes in me will live, even after dying. Everyone who lives in me and believes in me will never ever die" (John 11:25–26, NLT).

Speaking of the blessed hope that we have of Christ's second coming, Paul says that believers who have died, or "those who have fallen asleep in him", will be resurrected first. Believers who are still alive at that time will then be "caught up . . . to meet the Lord in the air" (1 Thessalonians 4:14, 16–17).

Paul describes this event elsewhere as a mystery: "We will not all die, but we will all be transformed! It will happen in a moment, in the blink of an eye . . . those who have died will be raised to live forever. And we who are living will also be transformed. For our dying bodies must be transformed into bodies that will never die; our mortal bodies must be transformed into immortal bodies" (1 Corinthians 15:51–53, NLT).

Losing a loved one can cause us to ask anguished questions about the state

of those who have died. Such a loss may remind us of our own mortality and undermine our sense of security in life. But Paul tenderly reminds us that we "do not grieve like the rest of mankind, who have no hope" (1 Thessalonians 4:13). As believers, we have the hope in Jesus of awaking to "be with the Lord for ever" (v. 17). May we comfort one another with these words!

[11] Kimberly Chia, "Farewell, as Inuka goes to sleep", *The New Paper*, April 26, 2018, 1.

If a non-Christian were to ask you to explain the hope that believers have in Jesus, what would you say?

In our bereavement, Paul tells us not to grieve like those who have no hope (1 Thessalonians 4:13). In what way might our grief be the same as the grief experienced by non-believers? In what way could it be different?

Day 16

Read 1 Thessalonians 5:1–3

Even when Jesus was on earth, His disciples already asked the question: "When will the world come to an end?" (see Matthew 24:3; Acts 1:6–7). Through the centuries, as early as AD 500, Christians have tried to predict the date of Jesus' return. Most of these predicted dates have passed.

While we may try to interpret specific world events as signs that Jesus' return is near, Jesus himself makes it clear that no-one knows which day or hour it will happen—"not even the angels in heaven, nor the Son, but only the Father" (Mark 13:32). Only the Father has the authority to set such dates and times, and these are not for us to know (see Acts 1:7).

In 1 Thessalonians 5:2, Paul refutes the claims of false teachers who were speculating about the time of Jesus' return. He reminds the believers that "the Lord will come like a thief in the night". Paul is not saying that Jesus will return in the nighttime; rather, he is saying that Jesus will return unexpectedly and swiftly, since no thief would warn his would-be victims about his upcoming heist (see Luke 12:39; 2 Peter 3:10; Revelation 3:3). We are always to be alert, because the day could come any time. Jesus warns us: "Keep watch, because you do not know on what day your Lord will come . . . the Son of Man will come at an hour when you do not expect him" (Matthew 24:42–44).

Unlike some pastors and teachers today, Paul did not see eschatology, or the study of end times, as an advanced doctrine reserved only for more mature Christians and theological elites. Rather, he taught everyone, even spiritual babes, "all the wisdom God has given us", in order to present everyone fully mature in Christ (Colossians 1:28, NLT). Thus, in the few short months of his ministry to the Thessalonian church, Paul had already taught his flock about Jesus' return and the "day of the Lord"—the time when God would come to punish the wicked and vindicate the righteous at the second coming of Christ (see Acts 17:1–4; 2 Thessalonians 2:5).

Christ's return is why Paul warns believers not to be worldly, indulgent, or spiritually complacent. We cannot fill our lives with the world's pleasures and let ourselves be lulled into a false sense of security. **Since Jesus is coming again, it cannot be business as usual for Christ-followers.** We must live in anticipation of Jesus' return, ever vigilant, ever expectant, and ever ready to receive Him. The day of the Lord is imminent!

What are the two figures of speech Paul uses in 1 Thessalonians 5:2–3 to teach us about the time of Jesus' return? What do these word pictures tell us?

If Jesus came back today, how ready would you be to receive Him? What have you done, and what do you need to do to be ready to welcome Him?

Day 17

Read 1 Thessalonians 5:4–10

No country is exempt from terrorism. Terrorist attacks can happen anytime and anywhere, suddenly and without warning. Governments, however, can do their best to be prepared so that they would be better able to respond if attacks occur.

Similarly, Paul reminds the Thessalonian believers to be prepared for the imminent return of the Lord. Continuing the analogy of the day of the Lord coming like a thief in the night, Paul notes that his hearers are "not in darkness" (1 Thessalonians 5:4). They were well aware of the imminence and certainty of Jesus' return because Paul himself had taught them about it. Spiritually, they also did not "belong to the night or to the darkness", for God had rescued them from the dominion of darkness and placed them in the kingdom of light (v. 5; see also Colossians 1:12–13).

Paul proceeds to remind the Thessalonian believers about who they are and how they should conduct themselves. As "children of the light and children of the day", they must behave like people who are awake in the daytime—watchful, clear-headed, not acting in secrecy or under the cover of darkness (1 Thessalonians 5:5–7). The apostle Peter, too, discusses being prepared for Jesus' return. "What kind of people ought you to be [in the light of Christ's return]?" he asks. Peter's response resonates with Paul's: "You ought to live holy and godly lives" (2 Peter 3:11).

Paul then offers a military metaphor of a soldier armed and ready for battle, urging the Thessalonians to be disciplined and self-controlled. They are to "be clearheaded, protected by the armor of faith and love, and wearing as our helmet the confidence of our salvation" (1 Thessalonians 5:8, NLT). The military image is one of Paul's favourite analogies for the Christian life (see Ephesians 6:10–18; 2 Timothy 2:3–4).

The Lord's people need to be protected by spiritual armour because they will face greater evil and increasing opposition as the Lord's return draws near (see Matthew 24:7–13). Commenting on the elements of this armour, Bible teacher Warren Wiersbe observes: "Faith and love are like a breastplate that covers the heart: faith toward God, and love toward God's people. Hope is a sturdy helmet that protects the mind. The unsaved fix their minds on the things of this world, while dedicated believers set their attention on things above."[12]

These three virtues—faith, love, and hope—form the familiar triad that characterises the "model" church (1 Thessalonians 1:2–3; see Day 2). Let us put aside sin, put on the armour of light, and be ready to receive the Lord!

[12] Warren W. Wiersbe, *The Bible Exposition Commentary*, vol. 2 (Wheaton, IL: Victor Books, 1996), 184.

What does the phrase "children of the light and children of the day" (1 Thessalonians 5:5) say about believers and how we are to live?

Reflect on Paul's analogy of spiritual armour—faith and love as a "breast-plate", and salvation as a "helmet" (v. 8). How do faith, love, and hope protect us? Why do we need to protect ourselves in this way as we wait for Jesus' return?

Day 18

Read 1 Thessalonians 5:11, 4:18

Today's headlines are testament to the chaotic world we live in. In the days ahead, we can expect to experience even greater difficulty and danger, for this sin-cursed world has been destined by God for destruction and re-creation (see 2 Peter 3:7, 10–13).

As Christians, we have the blessed hope of the imminent return of our Lord Jesus. We are destined for everlasting life with Jesus in a new heaven and earth, as described in Revelation 21–22.

However, we are not told exactly when it will happen. Paul did not teach about Jesus' return for us to argue and disagree over details concerning the end times. Rather, he taught it so that we might comfort and strengthen one another with the hope of our Lord's return (1 Thessalonians 4:18; 5:11).

What we know about Jesus' second coming is that it will be sudden and unexpected. Until then, we must learn how to live in a world ravaged by sin and evil, pain and suffering, death and disease. Thus, Paul tells the Thessalonian believers to "encourage one another and build each other up, just as in fact you are doing" (5:11).

The Greek word for "encourage" is *parakaleo*. Encouragement means coming alongside someone to give him the strength and courage to get up and get going again. It is like jump-starting a car whose battery is flat: you need to drive another car beside it to use its battery to charge the stalled car.

To encourage is also to give someone a nudge in the right direction. It is like giving a much-needed push to a toddler sitting on a stationary swing to get it moving.

In the Gospel of John, *parakletos* is used to refer to the Holy Spirit, who comes alongside us to be our "advocate" (John 14:16, 26). *Parakletos* is someone who helps, enables, or comforts another. It is difficult to find an equivalent to this Greek word in English, so it is translated in several different ways—as "Helper", "Counsellor", "Comforter", "Companion", or "Friend". These are indeed apt descriptions of a person who comes alongside us.

There will always be people who are feeling discouraged. You may become discouraged at some point in your life too. This is why Paul instructs us to "encourage one another and build each other up" (1 Thessalonians 5:11). His call echoes

Who can you encourage today?

another biblical exhortation found in the book of Hebrews, addressed to believers discouraged by suffering and persecution, to "encourage one another daily, as long as it is called 'Today', so that none of you may be hardened by sin's deceitfulness . . . and all the more as you see the Day approaching" (Hebrews 3:13; 10:25).

In what ways can your church, small group, or believing friends do more to show one another mutual love and encouragement?

Read 1 Thessalonians 5:12–13

God places us in a family of believers, a community of faith for our care, nurture, and mutual encouragement. This portrayal of the church as a family is important. Hence, at the beginning of his letter, Paul described the believers as "you who belong to God the Father and the Lord Jesus Christ" (1 Thessalonians 1:1, NLT; see Day 1). In the final 17 verses of this letter (5:12–28), Paul affectionately addresses them as "brothers and sisters" no less than five times (vv. 12, 14, 25, 26, 27, NLT).

Now that they have become part of God's family, the Thessalonian believers are to adopt the family's values and practices. Paul highlights three aspects of community life: leadership (vv. 12–13), fellowship (see vv. 14–15), and worship (see vv. 16–18).

Let's dig deeper into the first aspect today. Paul calls on the Thessalonian church "to acknowledge those who work hard among you, who care for you in the Lord and who admonish you" (v. 12). Although Paul is clearly talking about the congregation's leaders, he does not specifically refer to them as "leaders". Instead, he emphasises their hard work in caring for the community.

We are not sure why Paul wrote verses 12–13 in this way. Biblical scholar John Stott suggests that some members of the church may have been disrespectful towards their leaders. Or their leaders may have provoked such a reaction by heavy-handed or autocratic behaviour. "Paul rejected both attitudes", Stott notes.[13] In addressing the issue, therefore, the apostle distinguished the authority of the leaders from their service. The believers were to focus on their leaders' labour of love rather than their rank.

In verse 12, Paul makes three distinct points about leaders:

First, leaders "work hard". The Greek word for this phrase is *kopiao*, which is often used to describe manual jobs that require strenuous toil. Paul thus acknowledges that caring for a congregation can be arduous and wearisome. There is no room for laziness, half-heartedness, or sloppiness when doing work for the Lord.

Second, leaders "care for you in the Lord". Spiritual leadership is akin to parental caregiving; earlier, Paul had likened his role to that of "a nursing mother [caring] for her children" and "a father . . . encouraging, comforting and urging you to live lives worthy of God" (2:7, 11–12). Notice the qualifier "in the Lord"— the leader is qualified to lead the

flock only if he himself remains under the Lord's authority.

Third, leaders "admonish you". This is perhaps the most unpleasant part of pastoral work—to warn against sinful behaviour, rebuke, discipline, correct, and teach what is right. As the NLT puts it, leaders give the congregation "spiritual guidance" (5:12) in holy living.

Godly and caring leaders carrying out these tasks in the Lord, Paul says, are to be held "in the highest regard in love because of their work" (v. 13). It is hard for leaders to do their best when they are constantly being criticised by those under their care. We "show them great respect and wholehearted love" (v. 13, NLT) not because of their position, but because of their labour of passion and love.

This is why Paul calls church members and leaders to "live in peace with each other" (v. 13). Today, when conflict in churches often arises from tension between members and their leaders, such harmony is much-needed for unity to be maintained.

Does your church community appreciate and respect its leaders adequately? Why or why not?

What does it personally mean for you to acknowledge and hold your spiritual leaders "in the highest regard in love" (1 Thessalonians 5:13)?

[13] John R. W. Stott, *The Message of Thessalonians: The Gospel & the End of Time*, The Bible Speaks Today (Leicester, England; Downers Grove, IL: InterVarsity Press, 1994), 119.

Day 20

Read 1 Thessalonians 5:14–15

Fellowship has featured prominently in Paul's letter to the Thessalonians. In 1 Thessalonians 4, the apostle urged his spiritual children to keep loving one another and to do so more and more (see vv. 9–10). Now, as he concludes his writing with instructions concerning three aspects of community life (leadership, fellowship, and worship), Paul elaborates on whom the church needed to help, and how the church could help them.

Paul identified three groups of people in the church who were troubled and needed special care and attention—the disorderly, the discouraged, and the defeated (5:14). Let's take a closer look at each.

"Warn those who are idle and disruptive." The Greek word for "idle", *ataktos*, describes people who are not only lazy, but also irresponsible, disorderly, disobedient, and disruptive. Some within the Thessalonian church had rejected Paul's teaching and refused to work for a living (see 2 Thessalonians 3:6–15). Their ill-discipline and errant conduct disrupted the peace, and they had to be rebuked. Disorderliness and disobedience have no place in the Christian community.

"Encourage the disheartened." In contrast to the idle and disruptive, this second group of people were to receive tender care. The believers were called to come alongside and comfort these faint-hearted, timid believers who were frightened and despondent due to adversity. Perhaps some of them were grieving over the loss of loved ones and were unsure of their own fate (see 1 Thessalonians 4:13). Or they were anxious about their standing before Christ (see 5:1–11).

"Help the weak." The Greek word for "weak", *asthenes*, refers to people who are physically weak or ill, as well as people who are morally or spiritually weak. Perhaps they had not yet learnt to lean on the Lord for their spiritual needs. Until then, they needed strong support from the other believers. We are to "help", "uphold" (v. 14, NKJV), and "take tender care" (NLT) of such people, who may be spiritually exhausted or have fallen into sin.

These three groups of people need help not only from church leaders, but also from brothers and sisters. Pastoral care is also family care—one member caring for another.

Caring for one another in the family can certainly be challenging. It might be a slow, involved, and long-drawn process. So, Paul lists three attitudes that we need when we care for other members of God's family.

44

First, "be patient with everyone" (v. 14). Patience will ensure that we do not give up easily. It will also guard us from being harsh, critical, or judgmental.

Second, "make sure that nobody pays back wrong for wrong" (v. 15). The church is a forgiven community, and a forgiven person should be a forgiving person. A forgiving spirit will ensure that we do not put down those who stumble and fail, or those who are weak or wounded. Our willingness to forgive will enable others to receive and experience God's forgiveness.

Third, "strive to do what is good for each other and for everyone else" (v. 15). This is the guiding principle for member care: ultimately, to do what is helpful for each individual and the community. Galatians 6:10 expresses it well: "As we have opportunity, let us do good to all people, especially to those who belong to the family of believers."

Why is patience so essential when caring for the disruptive, the disheartened, and the weak?

What is one thing that you can do for someone who is in need of your help and care?

Day 21

Read 1 Thessalonians 5:16–18

As Paul concludes his letter, he seems to be giving instructions at random. But this is not the case—rather, Paul is following up on his call to the Thessalonian church to live in a way that pleases God (see 1 Thessalonians 4:1). Having urged the believers to honour their leaders and minister to needy members, Paul now directed their attention to the issue of Spirit-led worship.

All the Greek verbs that Paul uses in 1 Thessalonians 5:16–22 ("rejoice", "pray", "give thanks", "do not quench", "test", "hold on", and "reject") are what grammarians call "present imperatives"—in other words, they are commands. Today, let's look at the three commands contained in verses 16 to 18:

"Rejoice always" (v. 16). Paul commands the believers to be joyful at all times. But can joy be commanded? And what about painful circumstances in life when sorrow would be an appropriate response? Remember, however, how Paul pointed out at the beginning of his letter that the Thessalonian believers' joy was not dependent on their circumstances. Even "in the midst of severe suffering", they experienced "the joy given by the Holy Spirit" (1:6).

This joy is the Spirit's fruit, the outcome of living in step with the Spirit (see Galatians 5:22, 25). Having a relationship with God in Christ is reason enough to be joyful, for the Christian's life is one of " goodness and peace and joy in the Holy Spirit" (Romans 14:17, NLT). This is why Paul has no qualms commanding the Thessalonians—and us—to live joyfully. We worship and serve the Lord with joy because, as Christian author C. S. Lewis wrote, "joy is the serious business of Heaven."[14]

"Pray continually" (1 Thessalonians 5:17). This command does not mean praying non-stop or repetitiously. Paul instructs us in Colossians 4:2 and Ephesians 6:18 to "devote yourselves to prayer" and to "always keep on praying for all the Lord's people". Prayer is indispensable in worship, as passages such as Psalm 141:2 and Revelation 8:3–4 show. Conversing with God is part of both worshipping and communing with Him. This is why Paul himself punctuates his letters with spontaneous prayers (see, for example, 1 Thessalonians 3:11–13; 2 Thessalonians 2:16–17).

"Give thanks in all circumstances" (1 Thessalonians 5:18). Paul does not tell us to give thanks for all

circumstances, since some circumstances are evil and displeasing to God. Rather, we are to "give thanks in all circumstances". The Message renders this verse as "thank God no matter what happens". We are called to trust God at all times— not to depend on ourselves, but fully and only on God. This is God's will, because He knows that depending on Him is best for us.

Thankfulness to God is a distinguishing mark of a Christian, just as not giving thanks to God marks an unbeliever (see Romans 1:21). We can give thanks in all circumstances because we know that God is in full control of our every circumstance, and that "in all things God works for the good of those who love him" (8:28). When we become able to trust God this way, giving thanks in all circumstances would become part of our worship to the Sovereign Lord. Then can we say, as Paul did in Philippians 1:4, "In all my prayers for all of you, I always pray with joy."

Do you find it difficult to rejoice always or give thanks in all circumstances? Why or why not? How could you be more joyful and thankful in your prayers? What is one difficult circumstance in your life that you can thank God for?

Make a commitment to apply Paul's command to "pray continually" (1 Thessalonians 5:17). Reflect on what impact this will make on your prayer life.

[14] C. S. Lewis, *Letters to Malcolm: Chiefly on Prayer* (San Diego: Harvest, 1964), 92-93. Quoted in Matt Erickson, "C. S. Lewis: 'Joy is the serious business of Heaven', Renovate, Feb 13, 2019. Accessed from https://mwerickson.com/2019/02/13/c-s-lewis-joy-is-the-serious-business-of-heaven

Read 1 Thessalonians 5:19–28

grew up during a time of intense debate among Christian leaders about what were legitimate spiritual gifts, especially about certain experiences and practices. This debate continues today, reflecting an ongoing concern over how spiritual gifts are taught or practiced in churches.

It is likely that spiritual gifts, like prophecy, were also a source of debate and tension in the Thessalonian church, and her leaders had over-reacted, perhaps by prohibiting the practice of any gifts they were unsure about. This may have caused members to view all spiritual gifts—particularly prophetic utterances—with suspicion and "contempt" (1 Thessalonians 5:20).

Wrapping up his first letter, Paul calls for discernment. Believers must not quench the Holy Spirit (v. 19) nor reject Spirit-inspired prophecies (v. 20). At the same time, they should not be gullible and accept what is false (v. 22), but test all prophetic utterances and hold on to what is true (v. 21).

The Holy Spirit, the third Person of the Trinity, is also the Spirit of God and the Spirit of Christ (see Romans 8:9). We ought to relate to the Holy Spirit in the same way we relate to the Father and the Son. Jesus said that the Holy Spirit, the Spirit of truth, will

"teach you all things", "guide you into all the truth", and "tell you what is yet to come" (John 14:26; 16:13). We should not be afraid to walk with and be led by the Spirit, keeping in step with Him (Galatians 5:16, 18, 25).

We often think of prophecy as *foretelling* or predicting the future. But biblical prophecy is also *forth-telling*, "declaring the mind of God in the power of the Holy Spirit"[15]. God can give to some people a remarkable degree of insight into Scripture, into its meaning and interpretation, or into applications relevant to the contemporary world. Such wisdom understands the world in which we live, and helps us by expressing specific instructions for specific people in specific situations. Prophetic utterances exhort, encourage, and build up the congregation.

In this context, expository preaching—which focusses on what the Bible says and means, and applies its scriptural meaning to the present day[16]—is prophetic, because it presents to us the mind of God from the Word of God. The Word of God reveals who God is and what His will is for us, which is why we must not treat prophecies with contempt.

At the same time, Paul calls for caution. No one is to take any

In what ways might you be quenching the Holy Spirit in your life?

How would you apply Paul's instructions in 1 Thessalonians 5:20–21 to Bible teachings that you hear, watch, or read?

message at face value. **All teaching, however inspired they may seem, must be subject to critical appraisal.** Believers are to "test them all" (1 Thessalonians 5:21). As 1 Corinthians 14:29 puts it, they are to "weigh carefully what is said". Even Paul's teaching was not exempt from this principle. When he went to Berea to preach to the Berean Jews, they "received the message with great eagerness and examined the Scriptures every day to see if what Paul said was true" (Acts 17:10–11).

It is foolish and perilous to uncritically accept teaching just because a preacher is prominent, because as 1 John 4:1 warns us, there are many false prophets in the world. The NLT's take on Paul's words in 1 Thessalonians 5:21–22 is a good summary of a wise response: "Test everything that is said. Hold on to what is good. Stay away from every kind of evil." Or, in the words of one pastor: "Eat the meat, but spit out the bones."

[15] F. F. Bruce, *The Canon of Scripture* (Westmont, Ill.: Intervarsity Press, 1988), 264. Quoted in Timothy Lin, "How to Have the Power of God for Effective Ministry, Both Sacred and Secular", Biblical Studies Ministries International. Accessed from http://www.bsmi.org/download/lin/PowerOfGod.pdf

[16] https://www.thegospelcoalition.org/blogs/erik-raymond/what-is-expository-preaching/.

Day 23

Read 2 Thessalonians 1:1–4

A few months after writing his first letter to the Thessalonians, Paul received further news about the church he founded. It was a mixture of good and bad news. Returning to write once more, the concerned apostle began by commending his spiritual children for their steadfastness in the faith, before addressing the disruptive conduct that had arisen among them due to erroneous beliefs regarding the Lord's return.

Paul first deals with the good news. Having lauded them as a model church in his previous letter (see 1 Thessalonians 1:7), the apostle commends them again for their spiritual progress amidst severe persecution (2 Thessalonians 1:3–4). He also assures them that God knows about their suffering and will vindicate them (vv. 5–10). Finally, he challenges them yet again to remain steadfast and strong (vv. 11–12).

The believers in Thessalonica had suffered severely for their faith ever since they believed in Jesus. They continued to suffer after Paul left, as well as during Timothy's later visit. Their faithfulness to God amidst prolonged and heavy persecution was exceptional and praiseworthy. Not only had they persevered, but their faith was "growing more and more" (v. 3). Their faith had neither waned nor stagnated, but was flourishing.

It was not just their relationship with God that was growing, but also their mutual relationships within the community of believers. Paul acknowledges their progress, noting that "the love all of you have for one another is increasing" (v. 3). One who loves God will also love His people.

The Thessalonian church's radical loyalty and devotion to God prompts Paul to hold her up as a model for the second time: "We proudly tell God's other churches about your endurance and faithfulness in all the persecutions and hardships you are suffering" (v. 4, NLT). What a testimony!

How were the Thessalonian believers able to mature spiritually in adversity? Paul singles out the source of their stability and strength: the "grace and peace . . . from God the Father and the Lord Jesus Christ" (v. 2) which nourished their faith even in challenging times.

Grace and peace are both the gifts of the Father that come to believers through the Son and the Spirit.

Believers experience Jesus' peace: "In me you may have peace. In this

world you will have trouble. But take heart! I have overcome the world" (John 16:33). They also have God's promise of sustaining grace: "My grace is sufficient for you, for my power is made perfect in weakness" (2 Corinthians 12:9).

Paul rejoiced over the Thessalonian church's steadfastness, which was God's answer to his prayers on her behalf. "We can't help but thank God for you," he writes with deep gratitude (2 Thessalonians 1:3, NLT; see also 1 Thessalonians 3:12–13). God's faithfulness enables us to remain faithful, a truth which Paul affirms in 1 Thessalonians 5:24: "The one who calls you is faithful, and he will do it."

If Paul wrote to your church community, how might he describe your faith as a whole? Would he say that "your faith is growing more and more, and the love all of you have for one another is increasing" (2 Thessalonians 1:3)? Why?

How does your life reflect your spiritual growth? How has God's grace and peace helped you to grow?

Day 24

Read 2 Thessalonians 1:5–10

After commending the Thessalonian believers for their faithfulness, Paul now offers a word of comfort to alleviate their pain. He reminds them that God's justice is sure (2 Thessalonians 1:6), that He will relieve their suffering (v. 7) and punish their persecutors (vv. 8–10). Three points about God's justice are worth noting:

Commendation and reward. To comfort and encourage his hearers, Paul tells them that God is fully aware of their suffering and will act decisively in due time. "God will use this persecution to show his justice and to make you worthy of his Kingdom," he assures them (v. 5, NLT).

No situation is wasted in God's hands. He takes every circumstance—good, bad, sad, or painful—"to work together for the good of those who love God" (Romans 8:28, NLT). Their reward? To receive God's just vindication and commendation, for they would be "counted worthy of the kingdom of God" (2 Thessalonians 1:5). God will give them relief and rest from their suffering (v. 7) and they will "rejoice in that day and leap for joy, because great is [their] reward in heaven" (Luke 6:23).

Condemnation and retribution. On the other hand, God's just condemnation and punishment await "those who do not know God and do not obey the gospel of our Lord Jesus" (2 Thessalonians 1:8). God himself "will pay back trouble to those who trouble you" (v. 6).

God promises divine retribution against those who rebel against Him: "It is mine to avenge; I will repay" (Deuteronomy 32:35). Their punishment? To be "punished with everlasting destruction and shut out from the presence of the Lord and from the glory of his might" (2 Thessalonians 1:9). This judgment will take place at Jesus' second coming, "on the day he comes to be glorified in his holy people and to be marvelled at among all those who have believed" (v. 10).

Our just God. Paul's confidence is rooted in who God is (v. 6). Justice is one of the most celebrated attributes of God, as many characters in the Bible have attested. David proclaims that "the LORD is known by his acts of justice" (Psalm 9:16) and that "the LORD is righteous, he loves justice" (11:7). Abraham expresses his confidence that "the Judge of all the earth [will] do right" (Genesis 18:25). Job, too, echoes this truth in Job 34:12: "It is unthinkable that God would do wrong, that the Almighty would pervert justice." And Isaiah declares that "the LORD is a God of justice. Blessed are all who wait for him" (Isaiah 30:18).

In the midst of life's trials or unjust suffering, we can patiently trust our just God, our righteous judge. As the writer of Hebrews told suffering believers: "God is not unjust; he will not forget your work and the love you have shown him as you have helped his people and continue to help them" (Hebrews 6:10).

But those words of comfort also came with a challenge to persevere in the faith, in the very next verse: "We want each of you to show this same diligence to the very end" (v. 11).

How would knowing that God is just encourage and enable you to cope with life's challenges and injustice?

What does 2 Thessalonians 1:5–10 teach about Jesus' return?

Day 25

Read 2 Thessalonians 1:11–12

The Thessalonian believers had more than done well. Having commended them for their steadfastness and comforted them with God's justice (see 2 Thessalonians 1:1–10), Paul now challenges them to an even deeper walk with God (vv. 11–12).

Paul prayed continuously for them, as we saw earlier in 1 Thessalonians 1:2. Now, he re-affirms his commitment to intercede for them: "We constantly pray for you" (2 Thessalonians 1:11).

Asking God to do an even deeper work in their lives, Paul prays that the God who chose to save them would empower them to lead a life that is "worthy of his calling" by doing good works (v. 11).

Salvation is God's gift and can never be earned by doing good works. In Ephesians 2:8–9, Paul makes this clear: "God saved you by his grace when you believed. And you can't take credit for this; it is a gift from God. Salvation is not a reward for the good things we have done, so none of us can boast about it" (NLT).

While we are not saved by doing good works, we are nevertheless saved so that we can do good works. The great church reformer Martin Luther put it this way: "We are saved by faith alone, but the faith that saves is never alone."

Good works are the outward evidence that we are saved and that we follow Christ. God wants us to be "eager to do what is good" and to "abound in every good work" (Titus 2:14; 2 Corinthians 9:8). This is why Paul, speaking of salvation in Ephesians 2:8–9, sets forth one of the purposes for which God saves us: "We are God's handiwork, created in Christ Jesus to do good works, which God prepared in advance for us to do" (v. 10).

In 2 Thessalonians 1:12, Paul reiterates this point by reminding the Thessalonians that "the name of our Lord Jesus [would] be glorified in you, and you in him" when they faithfully did good to all. What a privilege to share in the glory of our Lord Jesus Christ!

There is more. When we excel in good works, God the Father is also glorified (Matthew 5:16). Both God the Father and Jesus the Son will be glorified. What an awesome outcome!

Leading a godly life by doing good, however, was not something that the Thessalonians could accomplish

by their own will and strength. Once again, Paul reminded them that only the grace of God could enable them to live a life worthy of Him. It is God who gives the capacity to do good works: "This is all made possible because of the grace of our God and Lord, Jesus Christ" (2 Thessalonians 1:12, NLT). What amazing grace!

What does a life worthy of God's calling look like? How would bringing glory to Jesus motivate you to godly living?

What is one good work you can do this week that will bring joy and glory to the Lord?

Day 26

Read 2 Thessalonians 2:1–12

To correct erroneous teachings concerning Christ's return, Paul had explained to the Thessalonian church in his first letter *how* and *when* Jesus would return (see 1 Thessalonians 4:13–18; 5:1–11). Soon after, however, some teachers began to teach that the day of the Lord had already come. Therefore, the persecuted Thessalonian believers concluded that they were now experiencing God's wrath on the dreadful day of judgment.

Paul identified three possible sources of the fake news—"a prophecy or by word of mouth or by letter" (2 Thessalonians 2:2). This false teaching purportedly came from Paul himself, making it seem authentic and authoritative. It not only "unsettled" many, but also led some believers to give up working for a living, a problem which Paul would deal with later (3:6–14).

Paul sought to correct this falsehood by reminding them of what he had taught previously (2:5). His purpose was always to pastor his flock, not to predict future events.

2 Thessalonians 2:3–12 may be one of the more difficult New Testament passages to interpret. But this teaching would have been clear to Paul's first readers, for he had taught them these things before, when he was with them (v. 5). They had heard about "the man of lawlessness" who would oppose God, exalt himself, and proclaim himself to be God (vv. 3–4). They had also heard about "the one who now holds it back"—a restrainer of some sort who would hold back the man of lawlessness until relieved of the task (vv. 6–7).

Because we don't know exactly what Paul taught them, it is impossible for us to know the identities of the restrainer and the lawless man. But of this we can be certain: the day of the Lord has not yet come, for certain key events are yet to happen (v. 3). Three events must occur, Paul notes, before the Lord returns.

First, there will be a worldwide rebellion against God: "That day will not come until the rebellion occurs" (v. 3).

Second, the man of lawlessness will be revealed. This "man doomed to destruction" will emerge from the shadows at the proper time to proclaim himself as God, defying and rebelling against God (vv. 3–4, 8). Whoever this man is, he is not himself Satan (v. 9).

Third, the restrainer—scholars have not agreed on who this man is—who hitherto restrained lawlessness and evil, will be relieved of this

responsibility (vv. 6–7). When this happens, all hell will break loose on earth!

Paul warns of evil and dangerous times ahead once all these events occur. The man of lawlessness will "use all sorts of displays of power through signs and wonders that serve the lie" and deceive those who are perishing (vv. 9–10).

But Paul also gives the assurance that God will not abandon His people—Jesus is in absolute control of the situation, and He will make all things right and good (v. 8).

Consider the three things that Paul says must happen before Jesus Christ returns (2 Thessalonians 2:3–12; see also 1 Timothy 4:1–2; 2 Timothy 4:3–4). What signs of the times do you see today that might suggest we are inching nearer to Christ's return?

Do you think that Jesus will come in your lifetime? Why or why not?

Day 27

Read 2 Thessalonians 2:13–17

Stability is a coveted quality in every sphere of our lives. We cherish political, economic, and social stability. Living in a stable environment is like sitting on an aircraft flying steadily through turbulence and assuring passengers of a safe flight.

In the spiritual realm, stability is not only desired, but also commanded (see 1 Corinthians 15:58, 16:13; Galatians 5:1; Philippians 4:1). Hence, Paul instructed the Thessalonian believers, who were buffeted by the strong winds of false teaching, to anchor themselves on God's truth—to "stand firm and hold fast to the teachings we passed on to you" (2 Thessalonians 2:15).

Paul had earlier assured his readers that they were "loved by God" and "he has chosen you" (1 Thessalonians 1:4). Now, as he urged them to remain steadfast, Paul reminded them to cling to the same unassailable truth of God's loving election and call. They were so "loved by the Lord, because God *chose* you as firstfruits to be saved through the sanctifying work of the Spirit and through belief in the truth. He *called* you to this through our gospel, that you might share in the glory of our Lord Jesus Christ" (2 Thessalonians 2:13–14; emphasis added).

The doctrine of God's election is much debated today. But as Bible scholar John Stott observed, this doctrine is almost always mentioned in Scripture for pastoral, practical reasons—"in order to foster assurance, holiness, humility and witness".[17]

That God "elects" people is seen in His call to Abraham, His choice of Jacob over Esau, and His selection of Israel out of all nations to be His treasured possession. Paul also says that "[God] chose us in [Christ] before the creation of the world . . . In love he predestined us for adoption to sonship" (Ephesians 1:4–5; see also Romans 8:28–33). That's why Christians are also called "God's elect" or "God's chosen" (Romans 8:33; Titus 1:1; 1 Peter 1:1).

God did not choose us because we were worthy. He chose us before we "were born or had done anything good or bad, plainly showing that God's act of choice has nothing to do with achievements, good or bad, but is entirely a matter of his will" (Romans 9:11–12, PHILLIPS).

Other verses tell us what lies behind God's choice: God "set his affection on you and [chose] you because . . . the LORD loved you" (Deuteronomy 7:7–8; see also 4:37; 10:15). And

Thinkhrough

"God saved us and called us . . . not because we deserved it, but . . . to show us his grace" (2 Timothy 1:9, NLT).

Although we were "chosen" before the creation of the world, our election by God becomes evident in our life only when we believe in the Lord Jesus Christ. The New Century Version renders 2 Thessalonians 2:13–14 in this way: "You are saved by the Spirit that makes you holy and by your faith in the truth. God used the Good News that we preached to call you to be saved." The Thessalonians becoming Christians was proof that God had elected them. For "all who were chosen for eternal life became believers" (Acts 13:48, NLT).

In encouraging them to stand firm, Paul pointed the Thessalonian believers to the truth that God chose them because He loved them. And this is the truth upon which we must anchor our faith.

[17] John Stott, *The Gospel and the End of Time–The Message of 1 & 2 Thessalonians,* (IVP, 1991), 31.

Why did God save us, according to Paul in 2 Thessalonians 2:13–14? What comfort and encouragement can we draw from this, especially when we are suffering?

Read 2 Thessalonians 2:16–17. What is Paul's prayer here for the Thessalonian church? How might his prayer apply to us?

Read 2 Thessalonians 3:1–5

Paul sprinkled prayer throughout his two letters to the Thessalonians (see 1 Thessalonians 3:11–13; 5:23; 2 Thessalonians 2:16–17; 3:5, 16). Praying for his spiritual children characterised his parental care. At the same time, the apostle also spoke of his own need for spiritual support. He was always ready to expose his own vulnerability, asking believers to uphold him in prayer (2 Thessalonians 3:1; see also Romans 15:30; Colossians 4:3–4).

This was a mark of Paul's humility. It reflected his respect for the believers and his dependence on them. Though he was a great intercessor himself, Paul was neither afraid nor embarrassed to ask for spiritual support from his spiritual children.

Notice that Paul does not ask his brothers and sisters to pray for anything that would bring him financial or material benefit. Instead, he focusses on the needs of his ministry and mission team: "Pray for us that the message of the Lord may spread rapidly and be honoured, just as it was with you" (2 Thessalonians 3:1). What mattered most to Paul was that the closed doors of human hearts would be readily and speedily opened to receive the Good News.

This was the burden of his heart and of his work.

Paul also asks the Thessalonian church to pray that he and his fellow evangelists would "be delivered from wicked and evil people" (v. 2). Wherever Paul went, people would oppose or even harm him to prevent the preaching of the gospel. This also happened in Thessalonica, where he faced such great opposition and danger to his life that he had to be sneaked out of the city at night for his own safety (see Acts 17:1–10). Just as "not everyone has faith" (2 Thessalonians 3:2) and wants to hear the gospel or believe in Jesus, not everyone wants the gospel to be preached.

Paul responded to these challenges by directing his hearers' attention to the Lord whom they all served. Echoing the petition in the Lord's Prayer to "deliver us from the evil one" (Matthew 6:13), Paul assures the Thessalonian church that "the Lord is faithful, and he will strengthen you and protect you from the evil one" (2 Thessalonians 3:3). He also echoes the assurance he had given to them in his first letter, when he said: "The one who calls you is faithful, and he will do it" (1 Thessalonians 5:24).

Then the apostle concludes his prayer by reminding his readers of

God's love: "May the Lord lead your hearts into a full understanding and expression of the love of God and the patient endurance that comes from Christ" (2 Thessalonians 3:5, NLT). Paul wanted them to remain steadfast, even as they waited patiently for Jesus' return.

Do you ask younger friends or your children to pray for you? How often do you do this? Why or why not? What do you ask them to pray for?

Jesus taught us to pray for deliverance from the evil one (Matthew 6:13). Do you think that Christians in general tend to neglect this important prayer need? Why?

Day 29

Read 2 Thessalonians 3:6–12

n 1988, Edgar Whisenant, a NASA rocket engineer turned prophecy teacher, wrote a booklet titled *88 Reasons Why the Rapture Will Be in 1988*. He predicted that Jesus would return to rapture the church sometime between 11 and 13 September, and that tribulation would begin on 3 October.

Over three million copies of this booklet circulated in the months leading up to September 1988. Taking Whisenant's predictions seriously, thousands quit their jobs and sold their homes in anticipation of Jesus' return. The predicted dates came—but not Jesus.[18]

Date-setters usually end up as up-setters: date-setting encourages impatience and restlessness, while discouraging productive living. This was what had happened in the Thessalonian church.

Misled by false prophets who said that Jesus had returned (see 2 Thessalonians 2:2), some believers had quit their jobs. After all, if the world was ending, why bother to work for a living? These people ended up living off the generosity of the church. The problem was probably only in its early stages when Paul wrote his first letter (see Day 14) but had since become more serious, threatening peace and unity in the community.

With so much free time, these freeloaders and loafers had become busybodies, indulging in gossip (2 Thessalonians 3:11).

So Paul had to deal with them more forcefully now. Twice (vv. 6, 12), he invoked no less than the Lord's authority (and not his own) to give instructions addressing the problem. The apostle commanded the church to "keep away from every believer who is idle and disruptive and does not live according to the teaching you received from us" (v. 6). The believers were not to have fellowship with freeloaders who disobeyed Scripture with regard to work and ignored Paul's example of working for a living (vv. 6–10).

This command seems harsh, especially as throughout the New Testament and in Paul's own writings, Christians are repeatedly instructed to be generous to those in need. But here, Paul is making a distinction between those who are *unable* to work, and those who are *unwilling* to work. **Those who cannot work due to disability or because no work is available deserve our help. But no help is to be offered to those who have ability and opportunity, but simply refuse to work because it is easier to depend**

on others. Paul gets tough on them: "The one who is unwilling to work shall not eat" (v. 10).

The church was to withdraw fellowship (v. 6) and withhold food (v. 10) from the idlers, for they did not deserve any help. Instead, these freeloaders had to find work and start paying for their own food: "Such people we command and urge in the Lord Jesus Christ to settle down and earn the food they eat" (v. 12). Instead of wasting their life, Paul tells them, get back to living in a purposeful and productive way.

[18] Dean C. Halverson, "88 Reasons: What Went Wrong?", CRI, April 20, 2009. Accessed from https://www.equip.org/article/88-reasons-what-went-wrong/ Stephen Witmer, "Stop Dating Jesus", Desiring God, June 27, 2017. Accessed from https://www.desiringgod.org/articles/stop-dating-jesus

What might have been the reason that Paul had to invoke the Lord's authority and not his own apostolic authority when dealing with idlers and freeloaders (see 2 Thessalonians 3:6, 12)?

Ceasing to work is one wrong response to the Lord's eventual return. What other responses do Christians produce that seem equally wrong or inappropriate?

Day 30

Read 2 Thessalonians 3:6–18

As an apostle, Paul had every right to receive financial support from the people whom he ministered to (see Matthew 10:10; 1 Corinthians 9:14; 1 Timothy 5:17–18).

Yet, the apostle chose to forgo that financial support from the Thessalonian church. He made tents for a living (see Acts 18:3) because he didn't want money to become a hindrance to winning souls. In his first letter, he reminded them of this: "Surely you remember, brothers and sisters, our toil and hardship; we worked night and day in order not to be a burden to anyone while we preached the gospel of God to you" (1 Thessalonians 2:9).

Now, in his second letter, Paul uses himself as an example as he corrects those who refused to work for a living (2 Thessalonians 3:6–10). In doing so, he also teaches the necessity of working for a living.

There is value and dignity in human work. In Psalm 104, the psalmist speaks of how God designed creation with functional efficiency; this was how God fitted all things together. Work has a natural place in everyday life: "Then people go out to their work, to their labour until evening" (v. 23).

Going out to work is part and parcel of creation's natural cycle; our work is part of how God designed the rhythm of life. God gave work to Adam as His gift: "The LORD God took the man and put him in the Garden of Eden to work it and take care of it" (Genesis 2:15). The fall did not introduce work, although it made work harder and caused it to be painful because the ground became cursed with thorns and thistles (see 3:17–19).

Even in Exodus 20:8–9, which contains the provision for Sabbath, we read of God's command to work. Many of us focus only on the day set apart for God, neglecting the fact that this one day of rest was contingent on six days of work—"Six days you shall labour and do all your work" (v. 9). Perhaps we need a radical shift from "Thank God it's Friday" to "TGIM"—"Thank God it's Monday"!

The Bible does not teach us to put our lives on hold to wait for the Lord's return. On the contrary, Jesus told His disciples to continue working and going about their business until His coming again. In the parable of the bags of gold (Matthew 25:14–30), our Lord reminds us of the mission entrusted to us: as we await His return, we are to be found faithful in doing the tasks He has given us. And when the Lord returns, we would

be able to hear Him say, "Well done, good and faithful servant" (v. 21)!

What guidelines for church discipline can we derive from how Paul dealt with the "idle and the disruptive" (2 Thessalonians 3:6) in Thessalonica?

Other than continuing to work for a living, what else should we continue to do as we wait for the Lord's return?

Going Deeper

in Your Walk
with Christ

Whether you're a new Christian or have been a Christian for a while, it's worth taking a journey through the Bible, book by book, to gain a deeper appreciation of who Jesus is and how we can follow Him.

Let faithful Bible teachers be your tour guides and help you draw closer to Christ as you spend time reading and reflecting on His Word.

JourneyThrough
Job
Christopher Ash

JourneyThrough
Hosea
David Gibb

JourneyThrough
Amos
J. R. Hudberg

Available from: **ourdailybreadpublishing.org.uk**

Journey Through
1 Peter

Why would anyone want to follow Christ when it brings suffering? Does it make sense to hang on to the faith when you might lose your job, or even your own life? The Apostle Peter addresses these questions and more in his first epistle. Journey through 1 Peter, and be inspired by God's grace and His glorious plans for us. Discover the value of pressing on faithfully like His Son, and strengthen your resolve to walk with Jesus through the pains and troubles of this fallen world.

David Burge is a pastor and teaches New Testament at Sydney Missionary and Bible College. His academic interest is in the life and theology of the Apostle Peter, and the ways in which Peter helps us to appreciate Jesus. He has written and published several books, including *2 Peter: Faith in a Sceptical World* and *First-Century Guides to Life and Death: Epictetus, Philo and Peter.*

Journey Through
2 Peter & Jude

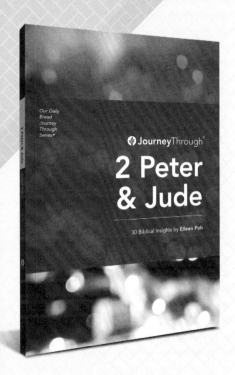

The early church faced challenges to their faith not only from persecutors outside their ranks, but also from those within. False teachers, as Peter and Jude repeatedly warned in their letters, sought to mislead believers and draw them away from the truths of God's Word. How can we guard against these same threats today? Journey through 2 Peter & Jude, and get fresh insights on how we can grow in the grace and knowledge of our Lord and Saviour Jesus Christ.

Eileen Poh was a lawyer for some years before doing full-time theological studies. Her doctoral thesis (at King's College London) examines the social relationships between Christians and non-Christians in Asia Minor in the second half of the first century AD. Eileen lectures in Biblical Studies at Discipleship Training Centre, Singapore. She is married to Philip Satterthwaite.

Available from: **ourdailybreadpublishing.org.uk**

Journey Through
Haggai & Malachi

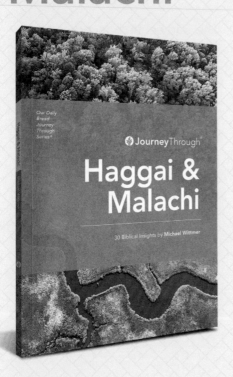

Life's hurdles and challenges can sometimes breed cynicism and smother our devotion to God. That's what the Israelites faced as they tried to rebuild the temple. But God did not abandon them in their despair. Instead, He sent prophets Haggai and later Malachi to encourage them. Take a journey through the books of Haggai and Malachi, and be encouraged by God's promises and love as you gain courage to trust Him with your disappointment and move on with hope and joy.

Michael Wittmer is Professor of Systematic Theology at Grand Rapids Theological Seminary and author of several books including *Becoming Worldly Saints, The Bible Explainer,* and *The Last Enemy.* He loves his wife Julie, their three children, and Asian cuisine.

Journey Through
Psalms 51-100

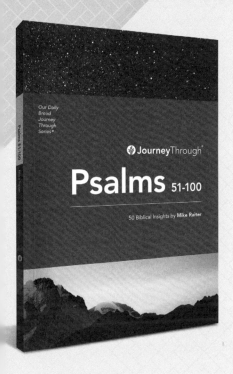

The book of Psalms is well loved by many believers, both for its uplifting songs of praise as well as its heartfelt words of lament and sorrow. Like a library of biblical truths, Psalms teaches us about God, salvation, hope, suffering, sin and obedience, the life of faith, the forces of darkness, and many other tenets central to the Christian life. Take a journey through Psalms 51–100, and rejoice, weep, and above all, worship our great God and King.

Mike Raiter is the Director of the Centre for Biblical Preaching in Melbourne. He is a preacher, preaching trainer, and former principal of the Melbourne School of Theology in Australia. Mike spent 11 years working in Pakistan, largely in theological education. He is the author of over 35 books and articles, most notably the 2004 Australian Christian Book of the Year, *Stirring of the Soul*.

For information on our resources, visit **ourdailybread.org**. Alternatively, please contact the office nearest you from the list below, or go to **ourdailybread.org/locations** for the complete list of offices.

BELARUS
Our Daily Bread Ministries
PO Box 82, Minsk, Belarus 220107
belarus@odb.org • (375-17) 2854657; (375-29) 9168799

GERMANY
Our Daily Bread Ministries e.V.
Schulstraße 42, 79540 Lörrach
deutsch@odb.org • +49 (0) 7621 9511135

IRELAND
Our Daily Bread Ministries
64 Baggot Street Lower, Dublin 2, D02 XC62
ireland@odb.org • +353 (0) 1676 7315

RUSSIA
MISSION Our Daily Bread
PO Box "Our Daily Bread",
str.Vokzalnaya 2, Smolensk, Russia 214961
russia@odb.org • 8(4812)660849; +7(951)7028049

UKRAINE
Christian Mission Our Daily Bread
PO Box 533, Kiev, Ukraine 01004
ukraine@odb.org • +380964407374; +380632112446

UNITED KINGDOM (Europe Regional Office)
Our Daily Bread Ministries
PO Box 1, Millhead, Carnforth, LA5 9ES
europe@odb.org • +44 (0)15395 64149

ourdailybread.org